FINDING DINOSAURS

STEGOSAURUS

by Samantha S. Bell

FOCUS READERS

FOCUS READERS

WWW.FOCUSREADERS.COM

Focus Readers is distributed by North Star Editions:
sales@northstareditions.com | 888-417-0195

Produced for Focus Readers by Red Line Editorial.

Content Consultant: Dr. David B. Weishampel, Professor Emeritus, Center for Functional Anatomy and Evolution, Johns Hopkins University School of Medicine

Photographs ©: Michael Rosskothen/Shutterstock Images, cover, 1; C. W. Gilmore/*Smithsonian Institution United States National Museum Bulletin* 89/Smithsonian Libraries, 4–5; Red Line Editorial, 6; Walter Bibikow/mauritius images GmbH/Alamy, 9; danku/iStockphoto, 10–11; Alizada Studios/Shutterstock Images, 12; Akkharat Jarusilawong/Shutterstock Images, 15; Peter Bennett/Citizen of the Planet/Alamy, 17; Linda Bucklin/Shutterstock Images, 18–19; Ed Andrieski/AP Images, 21; Hinrich Bäsemann/picture-alliance/dpa/AP Images, 23; Nicole Villalpando/TNS/Newscom, 24–25; James Woodcock/Billings Gazette/AP Images, 27; andersphoto/Shutterstock Images, 29

ISBN
978-1-63517-506-6 (hardcover)
978-1-63517-578-3 (paperback)
978-1-63517-722-0 (ebook pdf)
978-1-63517-650-6 (hosted ebook)

Library of Congress Control Number: 2017948069

Printed in the United States of America
Mankato, MN
November, 2017

ABOUT THE AUTHOR

Samantha S. Bell is an author and illustrator from South Carolina who has written more than 60 nonfiction books for children. She loves learning about dinosaurs and how they may have lived. She also enjoys being outside and digging in the dirt, but she has yet to discover any dinosaur bones.

TABLE OF CONTENTS

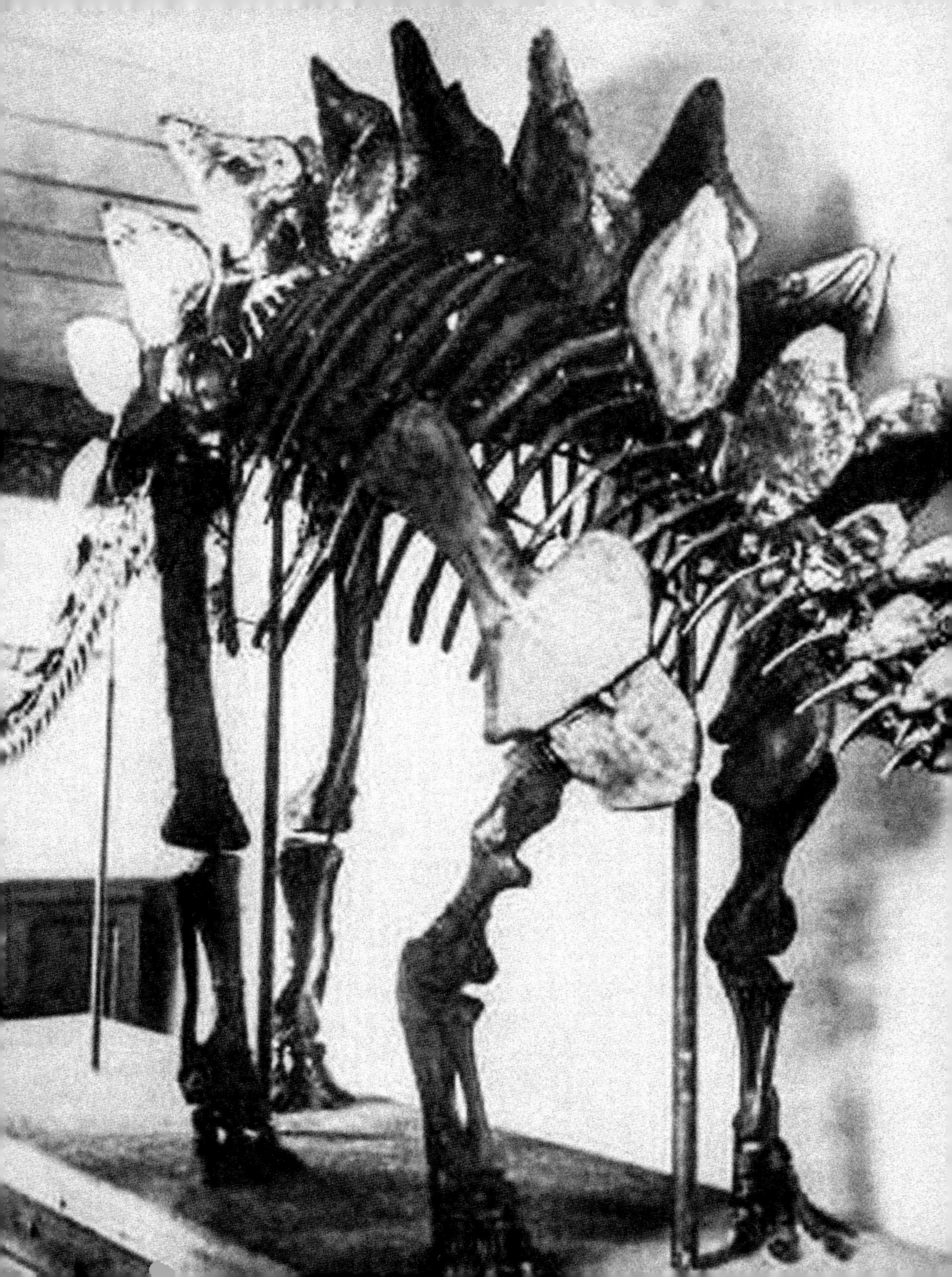

CHAPTER 1

A ROOFED LIZARD

In the late 1800s, fossil hunter Marshall Felch owned a farm near Cañon City, Colorado. The farm was part of the Morrison Formation. This area contained many fossils. In 1876, Felch was digging for dinosaur bones in a nearby **quarry** when he uncovered part of a skeleton. The skeleton included large plates and spikes.

Some of the bones Felch found are part of a skeleton on display at the Yale Peabody Museum.

It was unlike any dinosaur Felch had seen before.

MAP OF THE MORRISON FORMATION

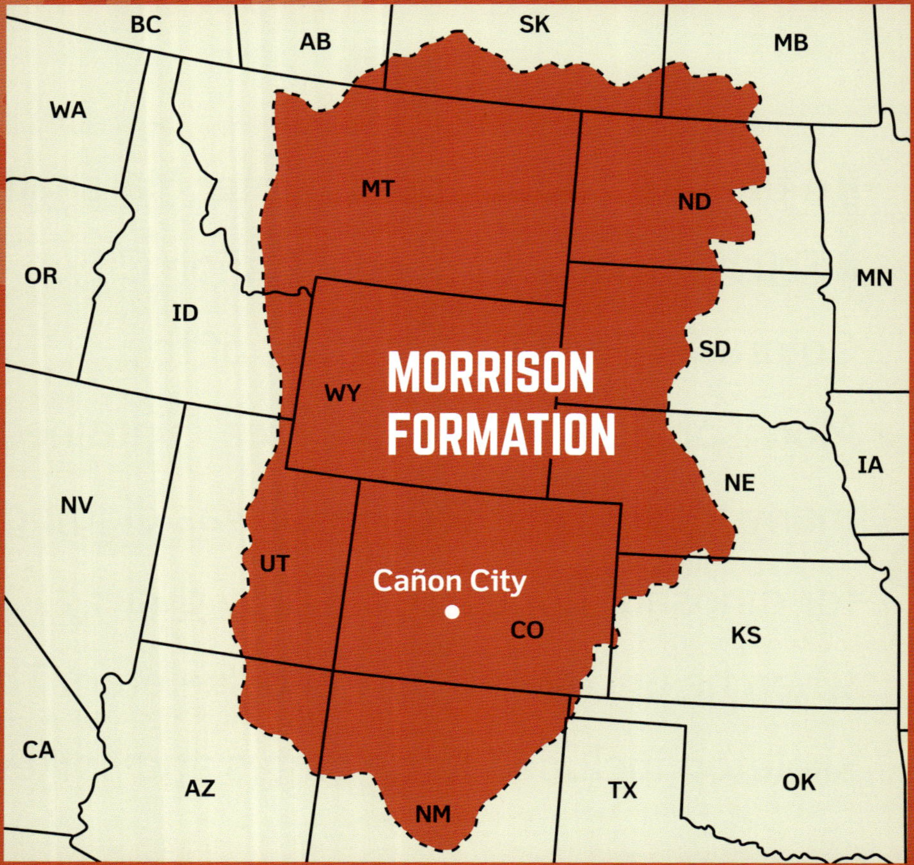

In 1877, Othniel Charles Marsh read a newspaper article about fossils in Cañon City. Marsh was a **paleontologist** who studied and named new dinosaurs. He sent a fossil collector named Benjamin Mudge to Colorado. Mudge spoke with Felch, and Felch agreed to send the bones to Marsh. Felch also continued to dig for fossils. He drew a map of the quarry to show where he found them.

After Felch sent fossils, Marsh worked on piecing them together. At first, Marsh thought the plates covered the dinosaur's back like a large shell. For this reason, he named the dinosaur *Stegosaurus*, which means "roofed lizard."

However, later finds showed that the plates had support along the dinosaur's backbone. Because of these finds, Marsh changed his idea. He concluded that the plates stuck up along the dinosaur's back.

Marsh was also wrong about the spikes. In 1880, he wrote that Stegosaurus's spikes were located on the dinosaur's wrists. Then a field worker sent him a sketch of the quarry where the bones had been found. It showed that the spikes were found near the tip of the dinosaur's tail. Spikes from other **specimens** were found near the tails, too. Therefore, Marsh changed his opinion by 1887. He placed the spikes on the dinosaur's tail instead.

The most complete Stegosaurus skeleton ever found had 19 plates.

Since then, many more Stegosaurus fossils have been found. Each new find helps scientists understand more about how the dinosaur looked and lived.

CHAPTER 2

PLATES AND SPIKES

Scientists think there may have been several different species of Stegosaurus. The largest species ever found is known as *Stegosaurus armatus*. This species was approximately 30 feet (9.1 m) long. The best-known species is *Stegosaurus stenops*. This species was approximately 20 feet (6.1 m) long.

There may have been as many as four species of Stegosaurus.

Visitors can view this cast of a Stegosaurus at the Senckenberg Museum in Germany.

A Stegosaurus's back legs were longer than its front legs. If the dinosaur walked too quickly, its long back legs would have passed its front legs. For this reason, scientists believe Stegosaurus moved slowly. Long back legs also meant that the dinosaur's tail was high in the air. Its short front legs would have kept its head close to the ground.

Stegosaurus had two rows of large, thin plates on its back. The plates grew from the dinosaur's skin. At first, some scientists thought the plates worked like armor. Then they learned that the plates did not lie flat. Plates that stood up would not have protected Stegosaurus from **predators**.

Research shows that Stegosaurus's plates were made of a bony material. But they were not solid bones. Instead, each plate had a hard outer layer of bone.

Inside this layer, there were blood vessels and **lattice**-like bone tissue. Because of this structure, some scientists thought Stegosaurus might have used the plates to **regulate** its body temperature. The blood vessels may have helped send heat out from the dinosaur's body.

Other scientists disagreed. They compared Stegosaurus's plates to the backs of crocodiles. Based on this study, they concluded that regulating body temperature was probably not the plates' main purpose. Instead, they thought the dinosaurs used their plates to recognize one another. The plates may have also helped Stegosaurus attract mates.

Paleontologists call a Stegosaurus's spiked tail a thagomizer.

Stegosaurus had four large spikes on its tail. Scientists still disagree about which way these spikes pointed. Some scientists believe the spikes pointed up. Others think the spikes pointed backward.

In 2005, scientists studied 51 tail spikes. Several of the spikes had broken tips. But the spikes also showed new bone growth. New growth meant the spikes had time to heal after they broke off. This showed that the dinosaur had survived the injury.

ALLOSAURUS ATTACK

One Allosaurus tail **vertebra** discovered in Utah had a puncture wound. This wound did not match the bite of another dinosaur. Instead, it seemed to be caused by a large, pointed object. Scientists created a diagram to show that a Stegosaurus tail spike was a perfect fit. This discovery provided evidence that Stegosaurus did use its tail spikes for defense.

Allosaurus (left) was one of the main predators that threatened Stegosaurus (right).

Scientists concluded that Stegosaurus likely used its spikes as weapons. The spikes would have helped the dinosaur defend itself from predators such as Allosaurus. Stegosaurus could have used its tail to slash an attacker's skin.

CHAPTER 3

HUGE, HUNGRY HERBIVORES

Stegosaurus roamed the earth during the Late Jurassic period. This period was between 151 million and 156 million years ago. Nearly all Stegosaurus fossils have been found in North America. But in 2007, one was discovered in Casal Novo, Portugal. This was the first Stegosaurus specimen found in Europe.

Stegosaurus probably spent much of its time grazing.

Stegosaurus did not live in large herds. But it might have lived in small groups. In 2007, scientist Matthew Mossbrucker found fossilized Stegosaurus footprints in Colorado. Some footprints were from a baby dinosaur. Others were from adult and **juvenile** dinosaurs. These footprints showed that Stegosaurus may have traveled in groups of all ages.

Because Stegosaurus's body was so large, it needed a lot of food. It probably ate for most of the day. Stegosaurus had small, rounded teeth. Its teeth could not tear meat. Instead, Stegosaurus was an **herbivore**. The dinosaur would have used its beak to pluck leaves.

Matthew Mossbrucker holds a cast of a baby Stegosaurus footprint next to an adult footprint.

Unlike many dinosaurs, Stegosaurus did not have strong jaws. In 2010, a scientist in Switzerland created a computer model of Stegosaurus's jaws and teeth. She found that its jaws could not break twigs or sticks that were more than 0.5 inches (1.3 cm) thick.

Instead, Stegosaurus could only chew soft plants. Because of its short neck, Stegosaurus probably ate plants that grew close to the ground. Its diet might have included ferns, mosses, and fallen fruit.

AN EXTRA BRAIN?

Stegosaurus had an open space in the vertebra above its back legs. For many years, some scientists thought a bundle of nerves filled this space. These nerves would have controlled the dinosaur's back legs and tail. This idea has been disproved. In 1990, a study suggested the space might have helped store energy. But scientists are still not entirely sure what the space was for.

A Stegosaurus's head was thin and pointed.

Compared to the size of its body, Stegosaurus had a small head. Its head was long and narrow. Scientists think the dinosaur's brain was approximately the size of a lime. That is quite small for such a large animal.

CHAPTER 4

STILL A MYSTERY

Stegosaurus died out at the end of the Jurassic period. However, many related dinosaurs known as stegosaurs survived into the Early Cretaceous period. Scientists are not sure why Stegosaurus disappeared earlier than these other dinosaurs.

Unlike many dinosaurs, Stegosaurus died out before the Cretaceous period began.

Scientists have several other questions about Stegosaurus. Some scientists have tried to estimate how much Stegosaurus weighed. But this is very difficult to do with only fossils. As a result, their guesses cannot be very precise. And even though scientists know Stegosaurus ate soft plants, they are not sure which particular plants it ate.

In addition, scientists are still trying to determine the purpose of Stegosaurus's plates. Some research shows the plates of males and females might have been different shapes. But it is also possible that the plates came from Stegosaurus dinosaurs at different stages of growing.

Scientists excavated a Stegosaurus vertebra and back plate in Montana in 2004.

Or, the plates could have come from different species of dinosaurs.

So far, no complete Stegosaurus skeleton has been found. Many of the fossils were found squashed flat. But with new discoveries, scientists hope to learn more about these fascinating dinosaurs.

STUDYING SOPHIE

In 2003, paleontologist Bob Simon found a Stegosaurus skeleton at Red Canyon Ranch in Wyoming. The skeleton was named Sophie, after the daughter of a man who helped purchase the fossils. Scientists are not sure if the dinosaur was male or female. But they do know how old it was when it died. The skeleton was almost fully connected. With 85 percent of the bones, it is the most complete Stegosaurus ever found. Studying these bones may help scientists answer many questions about Stegosaurus.

All of Sophie's skull bones were separated from one another. Scientists can study each one individually. The bones may reveal more about the dinosaur's eating habits. Computer programs can help reconstruct the tissue, such as muscles, that connected the bones. This allows scientists to study how the jaws moved during chewing.

Sophie the Stegosaurus now stands in the Museum of Natural History in London, England.

Scientists can also use X-rays and scans of Sophie's bones to create computer models. They hope to learn more about how Stegosaurus moved and how quickly it grew.

FOCUS ON
STEGOSAURUS

Write your answers on a separate piece of paper.

1. Write a paragraph summarizing the main ideas of Chapter 1.

2. If you found Stegosaurus fossils, would you keep the bones, give them to a scientist, or send them to a museum? Why?

3. Where were the spikes on a Stegosaurus located?

> **A.** on the dinosaur's back
> **B.** on the dinosaur's tail
> **C.** on the dinosaur's wrists

4. What could Stegosaurus have done if it had sharper teeth?

> **A.** It could have eaten thicker or harder plants.
> **B.** It could have defended itself against predators.
> **C.** It could have survived with less food.

Answer key on page 32.

GLOSSARY

herbivore
An animal that eats only plants.

juvenile
A young animal that is not fully developed.

lattice
A structure made of strips that cross one another.

paleontologist
A scientist who studies the ancient past and the fossil remains of ancient living things.

predators
Animals that hunt other animals for food.

quarry
A pit where stone is dug up from the ground.

regulate
To control the amount of something.

specimens
The remains of individual animals that show what the entire group of animals was like.

vertebra
One of the small bones that link together to form the backbone.

TO LEARN MORE

BOOKS

Barrett, Paul M. *Stegosaurus: An Extraordinary Specimen and the Secrets It Reveals*. London: National History Museum, 2017.

Hoena, Blake. *Everything Dinosaurs*. Washington, DC: National Geographic, 2014.

Lessem, Don. *National Geographic Kids Ultimate Dinopedia: The Most Complete Dinosaur Reference Ever*. 2nd ed. Washington, DC: National Geographic, 2017.

NOTE TO EDUCATORS

Visit **www.focusreaders.com** to find lesson plans, activities, links, and other resources related to this title.

INDEX

Answer Key: 1. Answers will vary; **2.** Answers will vary; **3.** B; **4.** A